SYCAMORE PUBLIC LIBRARY

W9-BVM-097

Published in the United States of America by The Child's World®
PO Box 326 • Chanhassen, MN 55317-0326
800-599-READ • www.childsworld.com

Copyright © 2006 by The Child's World®
All rights reserved. No part of this publication may be reproduced in whole or in part,
or stored in a retrieval system, or transmitted in any form or by any means,
electronic, mechanical, photocopying, recording, or otherwise,
without written permission from the publisher.

My First Steps to Math™ is a registered trademark of Scholastic, Inc.

Library of Congress Cataloging-in-Publication Data
Moncure, Jane Belk.
My four book / by Jane Belk Moncure.
p. cm. — (My first steps to math)
ISBN 1-59296-659-4 (lib. bdg. : alk. paper)
1. Counting—Juvenile literature. 2. Number concept—Juvenile literature. I. Title.
QA113.M664 2006
513.2'11—dc22
2005025694

My four Book

by Jane Belk Moncure
illustrated by Ellen Sasaki

SYCAMORE PUBLIC LIBRARY
STATE & MAIN STREETS
SYCAMORE IL 60178

This is Little  .

Little Four lives in the house of four.

The house of four has
four rooms.

Count them.

Every day, Little  goes for a walk.

Sometimes he goes to the zoo.

At the zoo, Little  sees three monkeys in a tree . . .

and one monkey on the ground.

How many monkeys does he see?

He buys four bananas
for the monkeys.

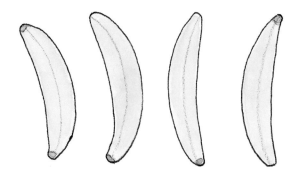

One. Two. Three. Four.

How many bananas
can he give each monkey?

Then Little  finds . . .

four balls

on the path.

He sees four seals in the water.

He throws the first ball to the first seal.

Who catches the second ball?

The third seal catches the third ball.
Who catches the fourth ball?

Next Little  sees some baby lions.

How many does he see?

Little  is happy. He claps his hands.

One baby lion runs and hides.

How many are left?

Little  hops to the kangaroo cage. "I see two kangaroos," he says.

Just then . . .

two baby kangaroos jump out
of their mamas' pockets.

Now how many kangaroos are there?

Suddenly, Little  hears a loud growl.

GROWL!

It is coming from inside a cave.

Out come two big polar bears
and two baby bears.

How many bears does Little  see?

Little  is excited. He waves his hands.

How many baby bears run to hide?

Then he stands very, very still.

How many bears peek out?

Little  skips along. He finds . . .

four peanuts.

Guess who peeks out of a door?

Does each elephant get a peanut?

Just then, Little  sees his friend the zookeeper.

She has a picnic basket.

"Come and share my lunch,"
 says the zookeeper.

"I have two sandwiches . . .

and two apples."

How many things does she have to eat?

After lunch, the zookeeper says,
"Let's have a treat."

Guess what she buys for Little 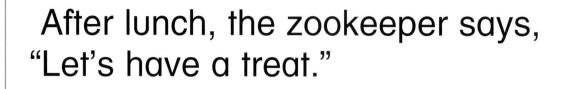?

How many scoops of ice cream does Little  get?

What does he say four times?

Little  found four of everything.

four monkeys

four baby lions

four kangaroos

four bears

four elephants

Now you find
four things.

Let's add with Little 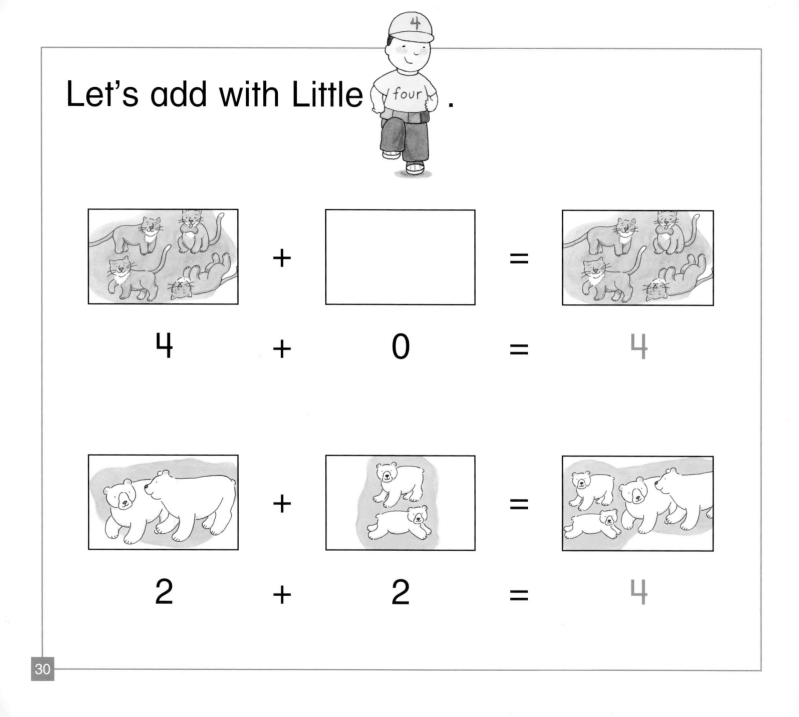 four .

$$4 \quad + \quad 0 \quad = \quad 4$$

$$2 \quad + \quad 2 \quad = \quad 4$$

Now take away.

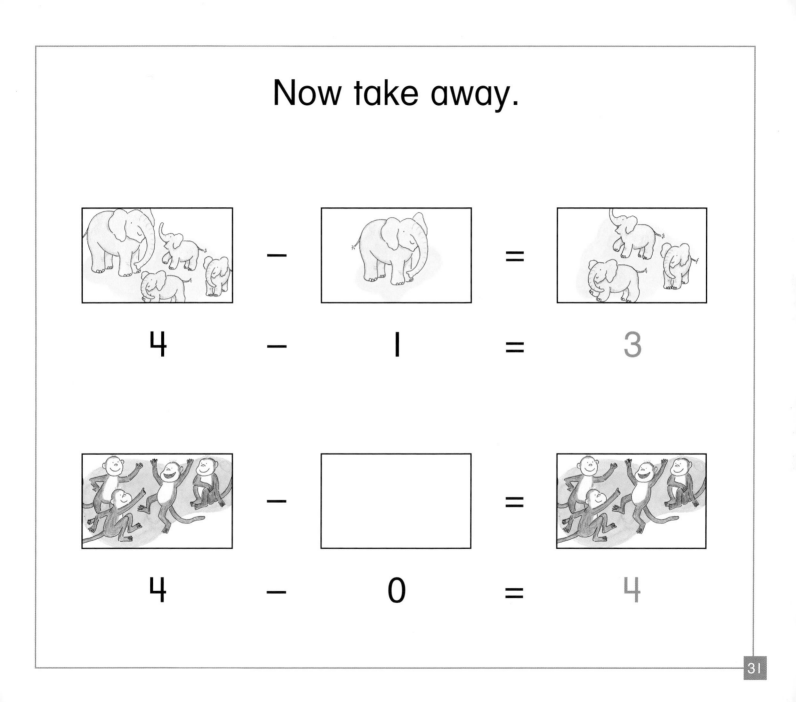

4   –   1   =   3

4   –   0   =   4

Little  makes a 4 this way:

Then he makes the number word like this:

You can make them in the air with your finger.